Symbols, Landmarks, and Monuments

Angel Island

Tamara L. Britton
ABDO Publishing Company

visit us at
www.abdopub.com

Published by ABDO Publishing Company, 4940 Viking Drive, Edina, Minnesota 55435.
Copyright © 2005 by Abdo Consulting Group, Inc. International copyrights reserved in
all countries. No part of this book may be reproduced in any form without written
permission from the publisher. The Checkerboard Library™ is a trademark and logo of
ABDO Publishing Company.

Printed in the United States.

Cover Photo: Courtesy of the State Museum Resource Center, California State Parks
Interior Photos: AP/Wide World pp. 4, 24, 27; California Park Service p. 11; Corbis pp.
    1, 6-7, 9, 10, 13, 14, 16, 17, 19, 20, 21, 23, 26, 28, 29; Getty Images p. 25; Library
    of Congress p. 5; North Wind p. 8; University of California, Berkeley p. 15

Series Coordinator: Heidi M. Dahmes
Editors: Heidi M. Dahmes, Jennifer R. Krueger
Art Direction & Maps: Neil Klinepier

Library of Congress Cataloging-in-Publication Data

Britton, Tamara L., 1963-
    Angel Island / Tamara L. Britton.
        p. cm. -- (Symbols, landmarks, and monuments)
    Includes index.
    ISBN 1-59197-832-7
    1. Angel Island (Calif.)--Juvenile literature. 2. Angel Island (Calif.)--
History--Juvenile literature. I. Title.

F868.S156B76 2005
979.4'62--dc22

                                                                2004050852

Contents

Island of the Angels

The sun rises over Angel Island.

Angel Island is the largest island in California's San Francisco Bay. It covers 740 acres (300 ha) and rises 788 feet (240 m) from the sea. From the island, visitors have a good view of the bay and the Golden Gate Bridge.

Angel Island holds a lot of history. Native Americans were the first people to live on the island. In the 1700s, Europeans discovered Angel Island. Later, the U.S. Army took it over.

In 1892, the United States built a **quarantine** station on the island. Soon, the government held **immigrants** there. In 1905, an immigration station was built to hold immigrants trying to reach the mainland United States.

The story of Angel Island is the story of America. Tales of immigrants blend with the history of soldiers who used the island to defend the country. But, the story of Angel Island begins with the Native Americans.

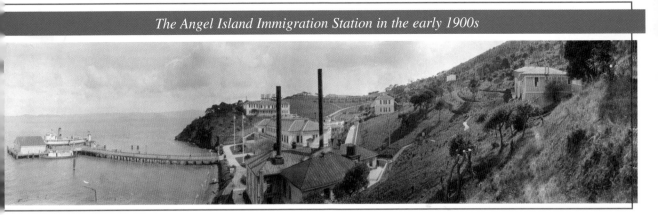

The Angel Island Immigration Station in the early 1900s

Fast Facts

√ The top of Mount Livermore, the highest point on the island, has been replaced. Now the island is 16 feet (5 m) taller than it used to be.

√ The South never made it to Angel Island during the Civil War. But, the battle that could have been is performed there for visitors every year.

√ The first ship quarantined on the island was the *China* because there was smallpox onboard.

√ By 1920, 6,000 to 19,000 Japanese picture brides, or wives chosen from photographs, were processed through Angel Island.

√ The average stay on Angel Island was two to three weeks, but some immigrants stayed up to two years.

√ The busiest month on the island was December 1945. That month, 23,632 men returning from World War II were processed there.

Timeline

<u>1775</u>	√	Juan Manuel de Ayala sailed to Angel Island.
<u>1839</u>	√	Antonio Maria Osio received permission from California's governor to build a cattle ranch on the island.
<u>1892</u>	√	A quarantine station opened for ships carrying diseases.
<u>1900</u>	√	The military changed the name of the army buildings on Angel Island to Fort McDowell.
<u>1905</u>	√	Construction began on the Immigration Station.
<u>1909</u>	√	Work began on an expansion of Fort McDowell.
<u>1910</u>	√	The Immigration Station opened.
<u>1922</u>	√	Fort McDowell became a military base.
<u>1940</u>	√	Officials closed the Immigration Station.
<u>1946</u>	√	Fort McDowell closed.
<u>1954</u>	√	Nike missiles were installed on Mount Livermore.
<u>1963</u>	√	Angel Island became a state park.
<u>1997</u>	√	The Immigration Station became a national historic landmark.

The First Islanders

Bark houses like those of the Miwok have been set up at the Indian Grinding Rock State Historic Park in California.

The first people to call Angel Island home were Native Americans. The Coast Miwok lived in present-day Marin County, California. They traveled to the island in boats they made from **tule** reeds.

On the island, the Miwok hunted deer, sea animals, and waterfowl. They fished and collected clams and mussels. They also gathered roots and nuts.

For years, the Miwok lived peacefully in the area. However, soon they would be forced to share their homeland. In the 1700s, Europeans began to settle on Angel Island.

A flower called Indian paintbrush grows in the traditional Miwok homeland on Angel Island.

New Arrivals

In 1775, Juan Manuel de Ayala sailed into present-day San Francisco Bay. Ayala was a Spanish explorer. He wanted to make a map of the bay. Ayala and his crew moored their ship in a small inlet on an island. Then, they set to work.

Don Jose de Canizares was a member of Ayala's expedition. He drew the first map of the area. They named the island *Isla de los Angeles*, which means "Angel Island."

Juan B. Alvarado was governor of California from 1836 to 1842.

Soon, other Europeans made their way to the island. In the 1800s, Russian otter hunters entered the bay. In 1814, sailors on the HMS *Raccoon* reached Angel Island. Their ship had been damaged and needed repair.

In 1839, Europeans came to the island to stay. That year, Antonio Maria Osio received permission from California's governor to build a cattle ranch there. His ranch had hundreds of cattle. But, war soon disrupted this peaceful period on the island.

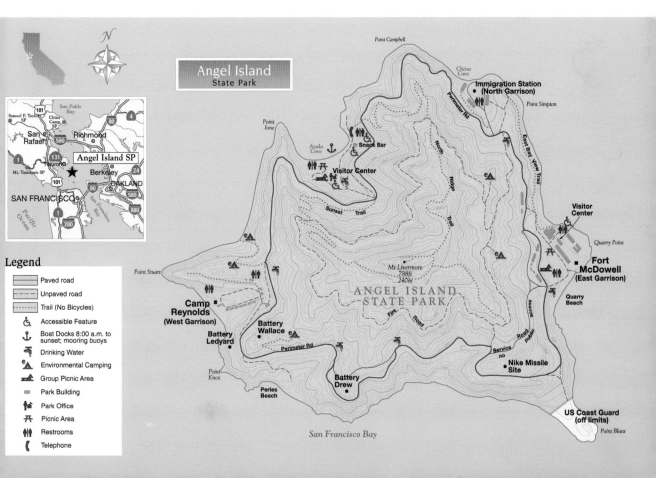

Angel Island
State Park

Angel Island SP

SAN FRANCISCO

Point Campbell

China Cove

Immigration Station
(North Garrison)

Point Simpton

Point Ione

Ayala Cove

Snack Bar

Visitor Center

North Ridge Trail

East Bay View Trail

Sunset Trail

Visitor Center

Quarry Point

Mt Livermore
788ft
240m

ANGEL ISLAND
STATE PARK

Fort McDowell
(East Garrison)

Quarry Beach

Point Stuart

Camp Reynolds
(West Garrison)

Battery Wallace

Battery Ledyard

Fire Road

Perimeter Rd

Service Road public

Service Road no public

Nike Missile Site

Point Knox

Perles Beach

Battery Drew

US Coast Guard
(off limits)

Point Blunt

San Francisco Bay

Legend

	Paved road
	Unpaved road
	Trail (No Bicycles)
🚹	Accessible Feature
⚓	Boat Docks 8:00 a.m. to sunset; mooring buoys
	Drinking Water
	Environmental Camping
	Group Picnic Area
	Park Building
	Park Office
🍱	Picnic Area
🚻	Restrooms
	Telephone

The Army Takes Over

In 1846, the United States entered the **Mexican War**. The United States won the war and took possession of California. Osio lost his claim to Angel Island, and the U.S. Army expanded its presence there.

In 1861, the **Civil War** began. Officials feared that the Confederate army would attempt to attack Angel Island. So, Camp Reynolds was established. There, troops guarded the bay against attack.

Government officials then saw a new use for the island because of its **isolation**. In 1892, a **quarantine** station opened on Angel Island. Sick troops returning from the **Spanish-American War** were isolated there.

Soon, more than just ships were quarantined on the island. For the first time, the island also became a stopping point for **immigrants**. To understand the immigrant experience on Angel Island, it is helpful to look at a little history.

Men in Civil War uniforms fire a reproduction of a Civil War cannon on Angel Island.

Coming to America

Ellis Island in New York Harbor was America's main **immigration** station. Most immigrants were processed there. But, Ellis Island was on the East Coast. It was closer for Asian immigrants to enter the country from the West Coast.

A drawing from the mid-1800s shows Chinese immigrants searching for California gold.

So, most Asian immigrants entered the country through California. They came from Japan, Korea, China, and other countries. The Chinese had been coming to the mainland United States since the 1840s. That was when gold was discovered in California.

Since then, many Americans had grown to dislike the Chinese **immigrants**. In the 1870s, the U.S. **economy** was weak, and Americans were out of work. Many blamed the Chinese for holding jobs they believed Americans should have had.

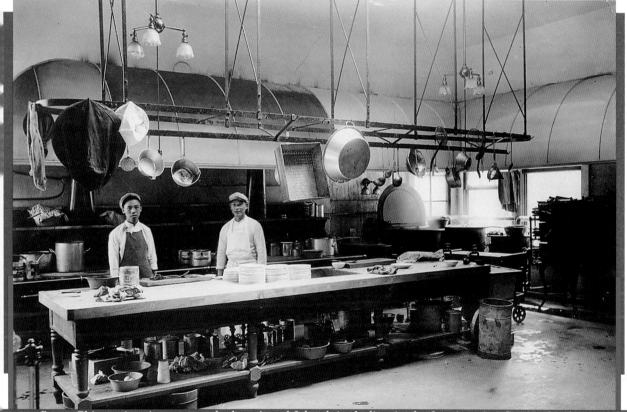

Some Chinese immigrants worked on Angel Island, including in the Immigration Station kitchen.

These ill feelings toward the Chinese increased. In 1882, President Chester A. Arthur signed the Chinese Exclusion Act. This severely limited **immigration** from China. The law had a ten-year time limit. In 1892, it was renewed.

Under the Chinese Exclusion Act, all Chinese immigrants were banned, with only a few exceptions. Teachers, students, church officials, and diplomats could immigrate. And, children of Chinese immigrants who were already U.S. citizens could immigrate.

The government wanted to make certain the Chinese immigration laws were obeyed. Officials needed more control over who was entering the country. So in 1905, construction began on an immigration station on Angel Island. The station opened in 1910.

Immigrant Experience

The journey from Asia to Angel Island took about three weeks. Ships first stopped in San Francisco. There, Europeans and first-class travelers could enter the country. However, most Asians were sent to Angel Island.

On the island, **immigrants** went immediately to the Administration Building. This was the building officials used to separate the immigrants.

After a medical exam, they were sent to the dormitories. Next, they had an exam with the Board of Special Inquiry. There, inspectors questioned immigrants about their pasts.

The Japanese on Angel Island

While the Chinese had a difficult experience on Angel Island, the Japanese were also trying to reach the mainland. Most Japanese were released from the island in two or three days instead of being held for months.

The Japanese women stayed on the second floor of the immigration building. The Japanese men slept downstairs.

As many as 60,000 Japanese on the island were picture brides. A picture bride married after sending her photograph to her future husband.

Japanese picture brides line up for inspection after arriving on Angel Island.

The poetry of Chinese immigrants, translated on the walls of the Immigration Station

Sometimes, Chinese trying to **immigrate** would make false claims. On their paperwork, they would claim to be related to a U.S. citizen. These immigrants were called paper sons or paper daughters.

Inspectors asked the immigrants many questions, trying to uncover the "paper" immigrants. Citizens that the immigrant was related to had to answer the questions in the same way. If the stories of the immigrants and the family members did not match, the immigrant could be **deported**.

During the inspection process, some immigrants stayed on Angel Island for just a few weeks. Others stayed for months, or even years. These were difficult times for them. To cope, the lonely immigrants sometimes carved poetry on the walls of the **barracks**.

The Writing on the Walls

Some of the poetry of Angel Island has been translated. Workers have preserved the carvings, such as the one below. The following poem describes the frustration of one Chinese immigrant.

Imprisoned in the wooden building day after day,
My freedom is withheld; how can I bear to talk about it?
I look to see who is happy but they only sit quietly.
I am anxious and depressed and cannot fall asleep.
The days are long and bottle constantly empty;
My sad mood even so is not dispelled.
Nights are long and the pillow cold; who can pity my loneliness?
After experiencing such loneliness and sorrow,
Why not just return home and learn to plow the fields?

More Military Moves

The military changed the name of all the army buildings on Angel Island to Fort McDowell in 1900. They were named after the **Civil War** general Irvin McDowell. The name of Camp Reynolds changed to the West Garrison.

The year before the **Immigration** Station opened, officials also began expanding Fort McDowell. The expansion included **barracks**, a hospital, a dining hall, and quarters for officers. Each month, 4,000 people passed through the island. They were going to and coming from the battlefields of Europe.

In 1922, Fort McDowell became the western base for soldiers shipping off to overseas duty. It was also where they returned home. By 1926, 40,000 men a year passed through the base.

During **World War II**, 300,000 soldiers left Fort McDowell for duty in the Pacific. While waiting to ship out, soldiers lived in the Immigration Station. German and Japanese prisoners of war (POWs) were held there, too.

Nazi supporters and POWs wait on Angel Island before being transferred to other holding places during World War II.

In August 1940, a fire destroyed the **Immigration** Station's Administration Building. That year, officials decided to close the Angel Island Immigration Station. In 1943, the Chinese Exclusion Act was **repealed**.

Fort McDowell closed after **World War II**, in 1946. But a new war soon began. The Soviet Union and the United States were engaged in the **Cold War**. Angel Island was again pressed into service.

In 1954, the military put Nike missiles on Mount Livermore. These anti-aircraft missiles were part of the nation's wartime air defense system. They were designed to protect the San Francisco Bay Area from foreign **nuclear** weapons.

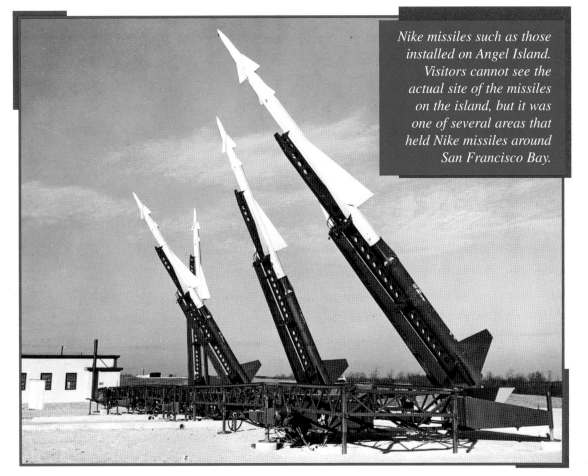

Nike missiles such as those installed on Angel Island. Visitors cannot see the actual site of the missiles on the island, but it was one of several areas that held Nike missiles around San Francisco Bay.

Preserving the Past

The missiles were removed in 1962. The structures on the island were decaying by this time. But Angel Island was not forgotten. In 1963, Angel Island became a state park.

In 1970, park rangers discovered the poetry on the walls of the **Immigration** Station. The rangers worked with the Angel Island Immigration Station Historical Advisory Committee to preserve the poetry.

This post exchange building is one of the abandoned sites that holds the history of the island.

In 1997, the **Immigration** Station became a national historic landmark. In 1999, Save America's Treasures donated money to preserve the poems. Californians voted in 2000 to spend $15 million to restore the abandoned buildings of the Angel Island Immigration Station. The project will cost about $30 million.

Lesson in History

Kids enjoy one of the many bike trails on Angel Island.

The **immigrants** who passed through the Angel Island Immigration Station made a long journey. And, they spent lonely days in the station. They hoped to make a better life for themselves and their families in America.

Today, visitors travel to Angel Island for different reasons. They rent bicycles, hike, or take a tour on a **tram**. Beautiful beaches offer an opportunity to sunbathe or look for seashells. Many visit the Immigration Station **Barracks** Museum to learn the history of the island.

The history of Angel Island symbolizes that of the country. There, the immigrant experience is literally written on the walls. These words are preserved for those who come to learn about the history of America's people.

A bell now marks the cove and beach that greeted immigrants after their long journeys.

Glossary

barracks - buildings that house soldiers.

civil war - a war between groups in the same country. The United States of America and the Confederate States of America fought a civil war from 1861 to 1865.

Cold War - a period of tension and hostility between the United States and its allies and the Soviet Union and its allies after World War II.

deport - to force someone who is not a citizen to leave the country.

economy - the way a nation uses its money, goods, and natural resources.

immigrate - to enter another country to live. A person who immigrates is called an immigrant.

isolate - to separate from other nations, societies, or peoples.

Mexican War - a war between the United States and Mexico from 1846 to 1848.

nuclear - of or relating to the energy created when atoms are divided or combined.

quarantine - when people suspected of having a disease are separated from others in order to stop the disease from spreading.

repeal - to formally withdraw or cancel.

Spanish-American War - a war in 1898 between the United States and Spain that ended Spanish rule of Cuba, the Philippines, and other colonies.

tram - a four-wheeled car that runs on tracks.

tule - type of reed that grows in wetlands. Tule is native to California.

World War II - from 1939 to 1945, fought in Europe, Asia, and Africa. Great Britain, France, the United States, the Soviet Union, and their allies were on one side. Germany, Italy, Japan, and their allies were on the other side.

Web Sites

To learn more about Angel Island, visit ABDO Publishing Company on the World Wide Web at **www.abdopub.com**. Web sites about Angel Island are featured on our Book Links page. These links are routinely monitored and updated to provide the most current information available.

Index